ELIZABETHAN

II

JONATHAN LOVEJOY

Jonathan Lovejoy

ELIZABETHAN

The Complete Poems of Elizabeth Peele

Volume II

Jonathan Lovejoy

Cover: *The Water Girl*, 1885
William Adolphe Bouguereau (1825-1905)

Elizabethan II

ISBN-10: 0692319174
ISBN-13: 978-0692319178

For every Elizabeth

Introduction

Carmen Angelina Coletti (Elizabeth Peele) was perhaps the greatest composer who ever lived. After her death, studies of her music revealed a body of work—almost exclusively instrumental—of such beauty and power as to defy description. Even so, her lifelong reclusiveness rendered them obsolete to the world, and these musical treasures may remain apart from public view forever.

Even those few who heard her original scores did so in quiet apprehension, that this beautiful widow—lost somewhere deep in North Carolina farming country—brought forth music as completely ingenious as any ever written before. The sounds of greatness flowing from this woman's piano, surely this is not meant to be! For what purpose can she truly serve as a neoclassical composer in a jaded modern world, except as a curiosity and eventually, a fountain of eternal exploitation?

But while music did serve as a profession for her since she was twelve—her only wage being a sound mind and spirit—there was still another expression, both private and unintentional, equally meant for her eyes only. Gathered posthumously, so few of these "assemblies" can be called unique or special, and likely cannot set her apart from any other lonely poet in the world. But still they live on, as a glimpse into the mind of a musical genius and abused woman of Faith. Written parallel to her music over the years—with no striving for greatness or immortality—these poetic trifles, ironically, may be the only compositions of hers the world will ever hear.

Elizabethan II

Jonathan Lovejoy

ELIZABETHAN

or

"The Assemblies"

Volume II

Elizabethan II

Jonathan Lovejoy

Such is the grandest music among us—

Poets…

Such are the wildest thoughts among us—

Composers…

The Book of Eve

28th Assembly

152

In our little world
In our place of isolation
There is no shame between us
Only pain

Pain caused by pressures of longing
Craving a life without fear and sadness
We are prisoners…two women
Living together alone

Bound by forces we cannot resist
Held captive in a prison
From which there can be no reprieve—
No escape from the pain of living

\

153

*H*igh above the night clouds
Where the moon shines without ambiguity
A white bird takes its last flight
Fading into history

A bird born of glass and metal
Flying with intrepidity
I rest devoured by its will and purpose
Braving through the misery

The bird flies onward through the night
Destination to nowhere
Speeding headlong into disaster—
Avoiding it miraculously

There is a magic cloth aboard
A window through the laws of nature
Ripping a tiny hole in space
Unequivocally

I place the cloth against the wall
Amazed by what there is before me
A gigantic wing of white and metal
Reaching to infinity

A sea of clouds glows dark and gray
Stretched into eternity

154

No wisdom can be found
In the carcass of a white horse
Cease the vain examination
And seek the truth where gospels be

From out of the Giant Tree Forest
A monster sings its hungry voice
Forcing us the flee to the plains
Where the mountain hill rises into view

Atop the snow capped mountain peak
A whirlwind appears in violence
Spinning snow into its funnel
Sending frozen rocks into the clouds

High above our plain of safety
Giant rocks fall from the sky
Seeking to destroy every one of us
Individually

155

She appeared to me from beyond the dead
Saying "you'll learn nothing from a dream, you see"
A woman who was cursed in unrequited life
Who left the world in agony

Loneliness on the serving floor
Bitterness for those deserving more
Darkness plagues from hill to shore
Hopelessness carried from times before

Children whose faces stare with quivers
Searching for a heart of empathy
Suffering torture by evil caregivers
Praying for a day of sympathy

She appeared to me from beyond the dead
Haunting my days of poverty
A woman who was cursed in unrequited life
Haunting the world in agony

29th Assembly

Jonathan Lovejoy

156

*T*hree souls adrift
On a Sea of Discontent
Looking to a far off horizon…
Hoping

One in Naivite
Blissfully unaware
Protected from days of poverty
Playing

Another in Virtue
Wistfully unaware
Exhausted by activity
Searching

A third in Wisdom
Miserably aware
Devastated by melancholy
Weeping

Elizabethan II

Three souls adrift
On a sea of discontent…

Waiting

157

A poor woman took a chauffeured ride
To a place she had never seen before

The poor woman rode a one way street
Looking for a place to go
She rode to the palace of a wealthy woman
To watch her act as rich women do

The rich woman said to "take a test"
To do as other rich women do
So the poor woman went to graduate school
To learn the ways of the well-to-do

The teacher spoke impatiently
Saying "you have no ability"
So the poor woman left the graduate school
With no knowledge of the well-to-do

A poor woman took a chauffeured ride
To a place she had never seen before

Elizabethan II

She left the class remorsefully
Waving apologetically
But the students had no smiles to give
Or cordiality

The poor woman sought to shake the hand
Of one student in civility
But the handshake cut her finger to blood
Necromantically

The woman tried to run for freedom
Stumbling frantically
She made it to her chauffeured ride
Panting exhaustedly

The poor woman rode the one way street
To the rich woman she had seen before
The rich woman said "you failed the test"
"Now take your place on the serving floor!"

158

Soul of deepest longing

My brightest belonging

Crashing waves upon a mighty shore

The shore of discontent

Harmonies breathe ingenuity

Bouncing diversity

Calling

Forming my soul's pleasure

A measure of desperation

Longing for a day of reprieve

Pain lurks underneath

Clawing

Hemming

Hawing toward final days

In awe of my spirit's

Blessed resistance

Elizabethan II

Standing firm
Upright in the Storm
Ideas make their own decree
Fading

Remembering the past
The place where clarity lives
Where Charity grows
Where disparity knows no bounds

159

The Power, I fear, is greatly diminished

I am left to feeble verses

Short trips across a breezy pond

From one shore of mediocrity to the next

The Grand Ocean, I fear, will lately be finished

I am left to failing shores

Where verses gather in waiting

To carry those of us who lose their way

Verses threaten to consume my days

A mountain of them

Stored in clouds high above

Words condensed

Coalesced

I would have traveled the Stormy Sea

From one shore of greatness to the next

But I wander the edge of this Grand Ocean

Hoping for another journey

Elizabethan II

Desiring

Waiting for a call beyond the sea

Verses have gathered high above me

To rain my wishful voyage away

Conspiring

160

A chirping tone

Songs from a hole in space

A gateway to another time

Another place

Whispers from beyond the sea

Laughter

Tears

Voices in ambiguity

A chirping tone

Songs for the present

Sorrow for another time

Another place

161

*A*t the carnival

I saw the boat ride swing low

Back and forth

Back and forth

The boat swung slowly

To a breezy rhythm

Backward and forward

Like a pendulum

The boat swept low

To a powerful swing

Onlookers crept over

To see the first woman scream

At the carnival

We watched the boat ride swing low

Back and forth

Back and forth

Jonathan Lovejoy

The boat swung upwards
Toward the sky
We wondered to ourselves
If it should swing so high

It swung to the ground
The riders screamed again
When it swept through the swing
It swung too high once again—

Malfunctioning technology
Sent the boat past its pendulum swing
The boat swung low and then high once again
Turning upside down

Shrieks and screams were everywhere
Four people slipped and fell to death
The boat swung back to its breezy swing
In rhythm once again

At the carnival
I saw the boat ride swing low
Back and forth
Back and forth

30th Assembly

Jonathan Lovejoy

162

When memories of the poison flow

Fear penetrates the mind

Cut him open and cut it out of 'im

The man is prepared to die

The man left a legacy of ten behind

When he braved the poison flow

He was dead before the men arrived

To haul his living body away—

When memories of the poison flow

Fear penetrates the mind

He lived beyond the final hour

Frustrated physicians told

He lived to pass the word to others

That he was prepared to die

Elizabethan II

Five sons among five wayward girls
Comprise his legacy of ten
In the midst of these is one at least
Who will never see his house again—

The children saw the man in pain
On the night he felt the poison flow
They heard him say "I'd rather be dead"
When his body fell to the poverty floor—

When memories of the poison flow
Fear penetrates the mind
It happened in the dead of winter
When the man was prepared to die

Cut it open and cut it out of 'im
The man is prepared to die

163

*B*eauty lives in white and lace

Inside the Halls of Poverty

Pain and memory haunt this place—

Beside these Walls of Misery

Apathy will hide its face

To abide these Calls of Agony

164

I prayed to the Heavenly Father
Keep the death stroke from my door

The death stroke came upon the clown
Twisting his mouth into a frown
It blackened his face from chin to crown
With no respect for his world renown

Pray to the Heavenly Father
Keep the death stroke from thy door

Jonathan Lovejoy

165

Regret filled his heart with a wish to flee

Away from a lifetime of debauchery

Righteousness became his new decree

Where sin and lasciviousness used to be

166

*B*ehind the white cold icy door
The mother stood in violence
Awaiting the knock to come once more
So she could lay the chilling words—

So she could say the killing words

The son sought entrance beyond the door
Where the mother stood in silence
The door was frozen from tip to floor
In a layer of ice and violence

He heard the mother call his name
From behind the white cold icy door
She said "never speak to me again"
Chilling him with words

Killing him with words

Jonathan Lovejoy

31st Assembly

Jonathan Lovejoy

167

From the clouds, a crystal falls to Earth

An ice crystal

A shape of unfathomable design

Whirling among billions

The crystal falls from the sky

Tossed on winds of chaos and bitter cold

Drifting, coming to rest

Upon a wasteland of winter white

There, it is quickly buried

Without ceremony or compassion

An irretrievable memory—

A frozen sea of regret

168

Flames erupted in the House of Worship
Games were interrupted by smoke and fire
The so-called Temple of God was burning—
Black smoke as thick as sod was churning

Winds blew through the smoke and ire
Deep orange flames burst into yellow
The Church of God was consumed with fire—
While blame assumed upon the Evil Fellow

Jonathan Lovejoy

169

*D*arkness whirls from clouds of fury

Devastation falls through amber light

Sunset calls forth the evening tide—

To show the funnel cloud in the dying light

170

The man chased the woman up the stairs
From the bottom to the top
He ran up behind her unawares—
Then she whopped him with a mop

When the mop flopped soap across his face
He groped to a sudden stop
He tumbled at an appalling pace
Then she stopped quick to call a cop

They hauled him to the coroner's place
Then she shopped in the Mall 'til she dropped

Jonathan Lovejoy

171

On the other side of rain

prosperity waits, hiding in ambiguity

bound inside the lust for passion

while time ticks away

in the halls of learning, people run to and fro

laughing

fighting like dogs

clawing like animals on the grass

women laden with sins lead men into corruption

corrupt men thrust themselves onto a scene in chaos…

a scene of battle

a war for sanity over madness

one walks among the insane

pilfering stilted murmering through life

looking for a time of peace

a peace of mind

Elizabethan II

understanding that no success will be given
only suffering, pain of a kind that cannot be imagined
there is a curse upon this wandering life
a power that holds men captive

some are a prisoner of privilege
some are privileged to fail
neither understanding how or why
only that it is what it is

and nothing more

be careful with the dealer
he knows how to dispense pain
without suspense...
on the other side of rain

172

On the night train

we seek Death nightly

politely we ask for its coming

to sprinkle magic upon our eyes

lightly

so that we may awaken from its touch

when the sun rises

then forthrightly, we awaken from our Death Ride—

on the night train

32nd Assembly

173

*t*he Glory of Heaven is so great

that life on earth cannot compare to it

like the flame of a candle

life's energy is lovely

fleeting

having its own purpose

but when compared to the Sun's power and brilliance

the candle's flame is diminished...

beyond comprehension

174

these make the world an evil place to live
bringing misery to every soul around them

upon the great lawn, outside the house of worship
the first drops of rain begin to fall
inside the brick house of worship
voices call in hypocrisy

screaming, whispering lies
disillusionment leaves the great hall
the church of riddles
where no goodness can be found

grief among the worldly elite
seeking a place to go
all acquaintances have fled to the hills
forsaking them they once knew

as the first drops of rain begin to fall
discouragement seeks a place of refuge
enduring stares of judgment, the mocking laughter
wondering where to go, to escape the coming rain

attempts to gain friendship have failed
leading to a world weariness
winds of rejection rise in the pouring rain
guiding

driving towards a new place of hiding
where the sun gobblers cannot see
a place of reclusion
seclusion

175

A voice synchronized with the ticking clock

Calls from behind the wall

Ticking away in an unknown tongue

I never knew at all

Chirping away

176

the world will listen to any slogan
hiding in the rib of a jessica

underneath the watery ground
the calf is buried to bones
without history or a future to bear
returning to the mud

lightning flashes
thunder explodes from above

177

*f*rom beyond the dead
the crone pushed through to say hi

scaring us

daring us to wave goodbye

mocking us

shocking us with her ugliness

a corpse

who was beauty in her past life

but is now the walking dead

Jonathan Lovejoy

33rd Assembly

Jonathan Lovejoy

178

His colors are the sky and the sea

The grass, and the leaves of every tree

These are the colors I long to see

Colors of life and liberty

179

When sorrow has been touched
we sing tra la la la boon-de-ay!

this is the path we have taken
the one most traveled through the blackness
in the everlasting darkness of Hade's Flame
there is nowhere left to go

spinning wildly out of center, housing difficulties
in spring's newest day
when the glow of futures has gone away
we sing tra la la la boon-de-ay!

from the mountain of corruption
peaks rising into the heights of misery
ranges that stretch back to the fall of man
rising above Eden's Horizon

where they could see the forbidden
invading their beloved home
when their sorrow was pushed into the evening
they sang tra la la la boon-de-ay!

new harmonies call from a distant land

where Padle's Crossing holds the sign of his coming

these are the last days

the end of the age is come

180

Blazing the winter like a comet's tail

Burns a trail of indifference

Who can care from one day to the other

Whether the sun will rise

In spring, summer, fall or winter

The sun burns over wickedness

High above in skies that threaten to be scorched

With nuclear technology

If plans continue

If the path chosen is kept

There will be fire where water ruled

In the days before

As it was in the days of Noah

So shall it be in the coming of the Son of Man

Fury blazing across time to infinity

From the beginning to the end of this age

And beyond

181

Every star across the night sky is an angel

Guarding us through the eons

Waiting

On the day of judgment the stars will fall

Flying to earth in a trail of fire

Covering the world in flame

Burning evil from their memory

Above a new earth

In a dark'ned sky

The angels will fly back to infinity

Becoming stars again

34th Assembly

182

Illuminating the need for the Redwood

a source of unending wisdom

seek no prompting from their world

rather let it flow where it may

boys are geese, flying to and fro

girls are marbles, rolling

brightly colored, beautiful

strolling in the wind

what comes in is like springtime

flown in upon westwind

lie in wait for your calling

your killing

the poisoning that your body has for you

pain beyond measure, beyond reason

agony from the ages awaits you in the melancholy flow

where death lives

Elizabethan II

there, it will carry out the cruelest fate
upon those who deserve a good life, a long life
but who had nothing but misery from birth
pain and suffering in life

then tears when they died in agony
and regret

183

Nothing would have gone fishing
nothing would have caught the line
at Sea Snake Edge
at Swampwoods Lane

applebows and buttercream misery
staring at the Chatham Trail
rootnelly where flash went into the lake
bottle caps hurl insane references

while the treesnake jumps at the tramp's opportunity
weep! call like an idiot in tune
toot thy own horn of destruction!
never mind where it all comes from

Chickalillies pop the marble skin, swirling discontent
Abram's knocking at the door, the door of thy darkest day
the heat finally goes off, so upstairs residents can breathe
while the downstairs rests in ignorance

there! the popping sound burns with what remains
ESCHATOLOGY is always the same
killing, mimicking the starburst trail, dying
lying to themselves while the struggle pays off

while the Arboretum is opened
spilling loads of flesh into the air
it happens above the mountain peak
where the Cold Flat lives and breathes with intrepidity

chiding stupidity, riding a wave of lost hope
it is bubblegum delicious, those words of discontent
these thoughts of malcontent, seeming to be nonsense
yet dripping heavy with meaning, and memory

Applebaum Lake is handy
resting cool upon the valley floor
with not a ripple on the surface
of grace and contentment

here, breezes swirl with warning
causing new ripples
activating the inclination to flee
away from WRATH

184

Melodies rise, rhythms fall

Harmonies call from beyond the sea

To hail death in all its glory

To savour the pleasure of dying

185

*N*øw, Bowler's Plane has been crossed
breached
reached by the maddening hoarde
the passing crowd of onlookers therin

Jonathan Lovejoy

186

Flying high among the elite
In awe of their ingenuity
In hopeful anticipation we meet
To fall from perpetuity

In the sky, our scaffolding breaks free
Plunging us toward the ground below
We tumbled downward helplessly
In too great a fear and pain to know

The elite fell down from high above
Plunging toward the ground below

Somewhere within our fearful fall
We saw a passenger balloon appear
It floated quickly towards us all
Transporting us 'til ground was near

Elizabethan II

We rested from our dreadful flight
To contemplate our miseries
Creatures crawled us into fright
Appalling our sensibilities

Drawing power from this elite
In awe of their ability
Knowing now what is replete
With fearful possibility

Jonathan Lovejoy

35th Assembly

187

In '91, when Mozart died

Where did his melodies go?

They drifted across the countryside

Above the streets of Pesaro

From VIVALDI into MOZART

To a swan the harmonies flow

In '92, when ROSSINI was born

There did the melodies go

188

*b*eware the tiding of the blue sword
hiding the truth in lying dreams
deriding the foolish and the simple
in their quest to know the way

one is cut by the sword at night
he tells her of his vision
she says "the sword means carry the Word"
to help his indecision

to help him to decide

twenty years of wandering to and fro
to the heights and depths of poverty
because of the tiding of the blue sword
they lived a life of pain

he preached and prayed to an early grave
because of a lying vision
he died inside the Winter's Cave
regretting his decision

Jonathan Lovejoy

she buried him in the
dead…
of…
winter…

189

The child was the size of a toddler elf
So it made me unawares
I let it climb down by itself
Then it tumbled down the stairs

The baby girl rolled down the stairs
Scaring me to infinity

The child went tumbling head over foot
Like a bouncing bowling ball
I thought the child had gone kaput
While I shrieked a shrieking call

I hurried down to where she lay
At the bottom near the hall
Knowing it was the Hand of God
That kept her in the fall

Jonathan Lovejoy

The toddler's eyes were clear and dazed
A bump was on its head
I could have not been more amazed
That she had not been dead

The baby girl rolled down the stairs
Scaring me to infinity

190

Underneath the Color of Night
Incompetence tries to build
Having no ability to see what's right
Until its feeble plans are killed

Bones lay across the ivory path
In full blown power of ignorance
Tones emboss the beauty of wrath
In the unknown hour of deliverance

Knowing proceeds upon the growing field
Sowing the seeds of confidence
Improving the path to the Harvest Yield
Removing the deeds of incompetence

191

Her friend sat in a courtroom chair
And lied in front of her face

When falsely, her friend made the accusation
What then, was the point of living?
When her friend lit the fire of indignation
Cynicism killed a heart of giving—

She died when her friend sat in a courtroom chair
And lied in front of her face

36th Assembly

192

The couple left the grocery place
They made a call in the dark'ned rain
Satan sat still in a nearby space
Watching them

The call was filled with anguish
The couple was filled with fear
Satan sat still in the dark'ned rain—
Watching them

The couple's future was in the air
The phonecall filled them both with pain
While Satan sat still in a nearby chair...
Watching them

193

Firstfruits of their deliverance
Laid casually upon the market floor
Great words of fairest independence
Awaiting delivery from sea to shore

Voices adrift in the Fall of Night
Calling forth their deepest pain
While evil watches with eerie spite
Drowning in the darkened rain

Jonathan Lovejoy

194

*N*ever consult familiar spirits
they lie in wait beyond consciousness
beneath consciousness
waiting to confound

to trick and to despise
the heart, souls and minds of men

try the spirits, to see whether or not they be of God
whether good or evil
whether they stand in the righteous plane
or in the plane of wickedness and sin

some seek to take over in this life
bossiness incarnate
getting in each other's way
seeking to be first in all things carnal

earthly

sensual

grabbing the stage even from the world elite

to take their place in the front row

where they dance and prance a jig of ignorance

still hating without cause

still despising

still denying their love for those who had sought it

familiar spirits

they lie in wait above consciousness

with unearthly wisdom

unearthly ability

now there is a wonder what can be done

to bridge the gap between knowledge and ignorance

there is fear that what was innocent is now abomination

and death

somewhere, there has to be a cry on this trip

a cry for deliverance

we won't see it that far

too wrapped up in the world not to seek

familiar with spirits

knowing if they be not of God

Neda…

bottolo bam dillyicious

arastic falls

remains of the littery

fear of whether the good has passed

to trust in Hosanna's Way

a warning to the little girl who has powers…

necromancy is evil

195

As I stand beneath the Seven Sisters
Gazing into sparkling light
I watch the earth stars blaze a trail
Across a fervent summer's night

Seven stars glisten through the ages
Above the rise and fall of men
As eons rule the Great Beyond—
Turning time and time again

I stand beneath the Seven Sisters
Underneath a fervent summer's night

196

*N*ow, snow becomes the death of civility

The death of good judgment

Invaders will populate the skies

With a warning that the end is near

Covering the whole world with hopelessness

These creatures know our weaknesses

Overseeing our demise

Understanding how to exact annihilation

The seas will foam from the arctic to the tropic

 Foaming poison upon the beaches, from the polar to the equatorial

To breathe the air will mean certain death

As though breathing borax powder

The aliens will walk among us

Unconcerned

Concerned only with our dying

Relying upon our feeble physiologies

Elizabethan II

The reign of kings will end
In the days of the poisoned snow
Days when man will cease his living
His killing

Now, the aliens walk among us
As the snow continues to fall
Unconcerned with the millions of families
The billions of lives underneath a layer of foam

Earth oceans lap at poisoned shores
Shores devoid of life

197

Think of the Hell thou wast delivered from

Dwell upon it

Know that thou hath tasted death

And survived

Learn that it hath no power over thee

Until thine hour is come

37th Assembly

198

The evening day

In the gloaming of gray

Time itself shall mourn

For every soul ever born

Weeping and sorrow

A bleak, hopeless tomorrow

In this evening day

In the gloaming of gray

199

*J*udgment appears in a dark'ned sky
Whirling from clouds of insanity
The Power of God hearkens a fervent cry
To write devastation onto humanity

A giant whirlwind flies to earth
Swirling from skies of mercy
Rain pours from the Clouds of Birth
Hurling lightning at Immorality

From inside the house of poverty
I saw the funnel cloud touch the ground
The black serpent twisted to and fro
Screaming a rumbling, thundering sound

I ran across the countryside
To escape the path of dying life
I saw the serpent devour a home
To lift a crying child to Afterlife

She was left to this unrequited life

In the rubble the child was pierced with a knife—

Released from the clutches of evil strife

Judgment could appear in a dark'nd sky

Whirling from clouds of insanity

The Power of God heeds our fervent cry

To write devastation away from humanity

200

Among heroes and legends

Lies a symbol of their greatness

Corrupted by time and neglect

Having value to no one

201

Someday

Race will fade to insignificance

Black, white, and every color in between

It will have no importance in the hearts of these people

Of this Great Nation

And for all of those who go therin

202

An ambulance lifted from a highway cliff

Exploding in the air

People gazed from down below

As though they didn't care

The fireball came from high above

Falling to the ground below

Plunging to the ground below

203

Through a false accusation
He sold his soul to violence
Seeking to kill those around him
Who sought to have his soul

He fought to escape their evil clutches
When the voice of their punishment rang
Though he deserved no day of scourges
One thousand lashes they pledged to him

They pledged to whip his soul to blood
To lay his body to the dust

Bewilderment flowed from a King's Carriage
As they sought to learn their grievous error
They approached the false accused again
Saying "we know now that you deserve only three"

Elizabethan II

They attempted to lash him three times one
Although they knew what he deserved was none
Their grip plunged him into animal fear
Confirming his weariness for these unworthy years—

Fear made the man attack and run
Though he should have had no pain to fear
But the officials covered the truth they knew
So they could blame an innocent

The truth must be disguised in silliness
If any can be expected to hear
They pledged to whip the wrong soul to blood
To lay their lying deceit to the dust

Jonathan Lovejoy

38th Assembly

204

When he hits me

It is there
In every corner
In every Shadow

The evil

205

On this side of prosperity
Poverty awaits
Taunting with corruption and bile
Threatening to take a life

In the classroom rests a dead path
Lost in perpetuity
Harmonies flow from the instructor's mouth
To add confusion to this delusion

A fusion of dying imagery
Pushes from the halls of learning
Escorting to the great lawn
To look for a place to rest

Ghosts of friends who are long gone
Drift among the corrupted hoard
There is no refuge for the weary
Among these trees of discontent

206

He called his sister on the phone
To give pleasure to a noisy woman
His sister listened in her home alone
While he pleasured on the noisy woman

She gathered lotion from her shelf
While her brother treasured the noisy woman
The sister pleasured on herself
While she listened to the noisy woman

207

The cop gave us the heebie jeebies
As he climbed the apartment stairs to me
Saying "Boy you've had your day of freebies"
"Son, you're going to jail with me!"

The cop was all of five foot eight
With a face like a Presbyterian Priest
He claimed I ran through the Garden Gate—
Though I'd not left home in five years, at least!

208

The clown fell down upon the ground

Blowing mounds of encrusted dust around

World wide wealth and healthy wishes abound

Where the sound of the clown's happy speech was found

209

Corruption is buried in the human heart

Like a seed

A young man
Walked among the young men in black
Having none of their lust for the violent life
Their vileness

Three from among the men in black
Gathered a circle around him
Who had no thirst for bile
Their violence

The young man's fear rose inside him
Rising like an evening tide
Though he tried not to be afraid of them
Their guile

The first blow struck him hard
Knocking him from his feet
They had no sympathy for the young man's fear
His life

210

The Cathedral Voices rose to a glorious clamour

An uproarious noise of nonsensical caterwalling

One Grand Voice of Self Praise, Self Worship and Self Aggrandizing

Screaming in another language

Unmusical

Joyously singing praises to the mile high ceiling

Rattling the windows

Rattling the ears of all who are present

A clanging in the ears of whatever GOD that may be listening!

39th Assembly

211

Even in the halls of poverty
Little girls have powers
Little boys cause hideous anger
Causing wicked canes to rise

Along the path of righteousness
A family is perverted in violence
An evil man and woman
Corrupting the children they bore

Screaming about future pain
Days of tar and wailing
Violence can often be found
Within the Halls of Poverty

212

A little boy threw water on the poverty bed
Enraging me to infinity

I planned to take to my sleeping bed
Outraged by what there was to see
I saw a mattress soaked in water
Enraging me to infinity

I chased the boy who did this evil
Hoping to break his neck in two
I raised a stick to beat him sore
Watching him cringe to the poverty floor

His screams brought the father from his accursed room
Bellowing in my ears like the voice of doom
Threatening again to wail me good
To flail me with a piece of wood

Like he had done before

213

"*Y*ou don't know what it is you've done"
The spirit said to me
Dwell upon the childhood images
From your days of poverty

Three hard knocks on the Door of Sleep
Saying "wake up from there, you sleepy head"
Days of rest are over and done—
Arise up from your poverty bed!

Elizabethan II

214

Yes, a tree grows in Brooklyn
Surrounded by days of poverty
Curtel and Vootel have been born
To be raised in days of misery

Drunkeness, violence, lascivious life
Nourish the children as they grow
They will suffer all the days of their life
Then its off to Heaven or Hell they go!

Jonathan Lovejoy

40th Assembly

Jonathan Lovejoy

215

*N*o man knoweth the day

Nor the hour of His coming

The sign of the rapture will be

When the moon is at perigee

Its closest place to Earth in space

Looking gigantic in the sky

A waning crescent light over dawn

Will stay to greet the rising sun

The moon shall turn to bloody red

Before it vanishes away

216

Earning it all through sweat and tears

Equality calls the River of Night

From the Land of Kings they braved the years

To give color and beauty to the Field of White

In chains they left their home behind

Spilling blood upon the foreign sand

Prophecy arrives their place in time

On the shores of a fair and distant land

217

Poe and Dickinson are these

Whose verse is worthy of world renown

But feeble verse will fail to please

Like pages of refuse hanging down!

Craft the words and let them go

With quality and precision

Never let those who claim to know

Impose upon your vision

218

The only thing that could be said
Is "the man faced blood in Crimson Red"
He whispered to me inside my head
The noise of a flood of Crimson Red

The man knew that soon he would be dead

Jonathan Lovejoy

219

$\mathcal{C}$lothesline wisdom fades through Dolly's way

Singing "oink! Oink! oink!"

Grasslands grown from the cricket's realm

Shading anthills from the sun

Whiddle lee dee thru Whiddle lee dum

Marcus O' Riley's pig has come!

Marchin' on thru to the preacher's drum

Waitin' for the dreary Spirit's Gum

41st Assembly

Jonathan Lovejoy

220

Children

Little bundles of emotion

Unformed clay

Unwritten pages

Lost souls

Waiting to be found

To be guided

To be shown the way to go

221

They danced a ballet in the Nebula Cloud

A realm of purple and gray silhouette

Spitting fire from the core of hatred

Inviting one another to die

222

I was touched by the ghost of a little boy

As I lay still under cloak of night

From in the midst of a troubled sleep

I felt a tapping at my feet

A tapping at my feet

223

A spirit arisen from the deep
Moved near to me and tried to speak
Saying "this is what you have to do"
"To make it to prosperity"

I listened for the Fated Words
But then the ghost was gone

Jonathan Lovejoy

42nd Assembly

224

A country crooner showed the Song of Light

Blazing colors against the wall

He changed himself into another

That I did not expect at all

225

Lullabye, and goodnight
Go to sleep, you little devil
I despise you with all my heart
I wish you had never been born

If I could go back in time
To when your father asked me out
I would laugh right in his face
And ask him, "please go away"

My little precious

226

Blot the blight on the paper

If it gets into your way

Or write around this obstacle

And say what you have to say

Hours, weeks, or years

What does it matter how long you stay?

Your idea will find completion

In its own appointed day

In its own anointed way

227

$\mathcal{B}$less the dear woman's right to choose

Those unaborted will be cursed with life

To be born is to be cursed

And to live is to suffer

Jonathan Lovejoy

43rd Assembly

228

The soap is orange

Yet the water turns green with envy

What toxic magic hath wrought this?

A clean, chemical miracle!

229

Are ghosts angels?

Demons?

Perhaps there is no suffering for the dead

Beyond the Gates of Hell

Is there really paradise in death?

Beyond the Gates of Heaven?

230

Calling for the April Rain
Futures from gray skies to weep
Heaven reveals the healing years
Underneath a Flowering Tree

Voices in the falling rain
Beyond the Sea of Destiny
Whispering a promise to where I stand
To wait beneath the Flowering Tree

Souls hearken to a Voice of Beauty
Adrift from far beyond the sea
Mercy falleth as Gentle Rain
Underneath a Flowering Tree

231

I asked the man behind the counter
To give me a word from the future
He rolled a waggle of potatoes at me
Angrily

Saying "Do not concern yourself with tomorrow—
Dinner should be your greatest worry.
Now, cook!
Eat!"

232

At night, in the House of Poverty
A boy rolled out from his sleeping bed
Strolling to his mother's room
Running from the dread

He woke her up from her weeping bed
"I can't do it anymore…
There're too many noises in my room
And voices from the dead"

233

Winds drift through mournful days
Wishing a whisper to a watery grave
Redemption cries these showers of spring
To soothe my aching sorrow away

I heard the rising wind speak through the trees
I saw a fervent rain from stormy skies
Teardrops gather in the pouring rain
Scattering melancholy at my feet

Jonathan Lovejoy

44th Assembly

234

It is the pleasure of kings

To hold others down in poverty

It is the measure of things

To have one's dreams crushed to nothing

235

From the hall of kings

Words fly in with the raven

Words of profound negativity

With pain for a broken spirit

236

Rest easy in thy grave

Thy tomb

Go gently to the dust…

From whence thou came

237

When I close my eyes

Ghosts appear

Flowing strands of music…

Haunting

Jonathan Lovejoy

238

Confusion rides the Train to Nowhere

While delusion speaks of safety

Tears flow from eyes of arrogance

And all riders of the train

239

Revelation cannot be denied

Understanding will not falter

Altered plans must be made

When futility is made plain

Jonathan Lovejoy

45th Assembly

Jonathan Lovejoy

240

Evil lives inside the looking glass
Innocence lost
The image of a dead little girl
Lives inside the mirror

The girl in the well is drowned
Thrown in by a mother's insanity
The girl reaches up from a watery grave
To hide inside the mirror

241

SIX have changed the Modern World

To make it a better place to be

Now they are called to a better life

Away from public scrutiny

Six are called to a quiet life…

A private destiny

Jonathan Lovejoy

242

Two travelers on the Road of Life
Speeding towards their destiny
One from the Wealthen Field of Dreams
The other from the Land of Poverty

Searching for a place to rest
Grieving for a Land of Plenty

243

Divas from another age
With beautiful ability
Sing the aria to persuade
A modern sensibility

Jonathan Lovejoy

46th Assembly

Jonathan Lovejoy

244

On this side of freedom

Rests a poverty room

The other side boasts a room of prosperity

A place of hope

With other spirits of the dead

I sit inside the poverty room

Without hope

Without a future

Knowing that success cannot be obtained

Only given

Even while the rose is in bloom

My life has withered away

245

There is an ugliness about me—
That I find revolting
I look in the mirror at myself—
Sickened

Jonathan Lovejoy

246

Mysterious harmonies begin to flow

A calling from beyond the sea

Years of prophecy come and go

Fulfillment of a Divine Decree

247

i am weary in this life

tired of curses

unanswered prayers

misery

through the waking hours i suffer

then i wander through the Land of the Dead

where evil spirits live

spirits with no compassion

pain from the waking hours

carried over

in the Land of the Dead

i see the pain of my life in form…

compounded

rejection…

mocking, loathing

vengeance, envy

failure

visions of others who do not suffer

pain from the waking hours
carried over

there may be no other course
for this unrequited life
except a return to the Land of the Dead
indefinitely

where pain from the waking hours
is carried over

248

In the dark place

Sickness awaits

To contaminate the body

With disease, pain…

And death

Jonathan Lovejoy

47th Assembly

249

*M*en have the glory

In this world

WOMEN

Have the power

250

I so rarely see the sky
Except it be through a window
A sea of azure blue
With clouds of fluffy white

My mind soars
Through the window of my prison
Flying high on wings of freedom…
Drifting

Across a Cerulean Sea
Through clouds high above me
A plane travels to its lonely destination
Somewhere

251

May Heaven forgive us

For the lies we must tell

To save the feelings of another

To keep the peace

Turn away wrath and pain

With a kind word

48th Assembly

Jonathan Lovejoy

252

While trimming the tree on Christmas Eve

I heard a knocking at the door

A woman appeared on the other side

An image I had seen before…

The woman was my grandmother

From when she was only 44!

253

Streams of consciousness
Leave me on the poverty floor
Resting upon the dust linen
Waiting to be born

Conformity has its place
Upon the raft of Kliner's Payne
Recline in thine office bay
To stay out of the rain

Racked with disease and injury
Where the soul goes to die
Wrapped in diligent Fervor's Mane
Explaining carnality

Where has this past arisen
Fortuitous in the madness game
Virginia's Nest is filled with tears
Painfully

Jonathan Lovejoy

Strings and strands of irritation

Reds bouncing on rhythms of excruciation

Running to and fro

Going to nowhere

One more step to apocalypse

Flowing from beyond

Whirling clouds in graying cloak

Coated with devastation

Destruction is his calling

His destiny

254

Violent kisses confound the spirit

Creating desire

Lustful

Carnal

Look towards the times

To see the sign of His coming

Be lost in the search for it

The waiting

255

In the world of broken dreams
Barriers rise in the land before me
As rain falls from gray skies
I am lost

I gather what strength there is
To seek another way
But the road to life and freedom
Is hidden

Wandering these dark roads
Rain soaked streets of poverty
Wondering if I will ever see…
Hope and Prosperity

49th Assembly

256

I want to go outside
I long to walk the Fields of Plenty
Away from these walls
This prison

When I see trees blowing in the wind
When I see birds flying high in the sky
I long for what they take for granted
I long for it

257

Lightning strikes my nerves!
Thunder rattles me to the core!
Confusion twists me like a coil!
Panic!

Jonathan Lovejoy

258

Oboes intertwined
Upon the Harvest Trail
Tales of wind from another Time
Another history

Another place of strings
Cellos whisper velvetine tones
Soothing the violin's apprehension
Tensions for the viola's pain

Basses booming
Timpani's looming a stormy rumble
Tumbling trombones whirling through
A brass ring of fire

Horns call from another place
Coloring each key among them
Saving grace from the ordinary
In ambiguity

Elizabethan II

En masse each voice in Tutti's Call
Rising above the voices of chatterly
Singing songs of glory's way
Days of beauty and frolicking

Rolicking times of grandeur
Feeling across the Barrier Land
Getting lost along the way
To rhythmic perfection

Detection saves each waning section
Allowing seams to mend
Harmonies blend with the air itself
Wishing

Longing for appreciation
Hoping for a better time

50th Assembly

Jonathan Lovejoy

259

As they begin a new journey
Two meet in the Dark World
Dreading the future awaiting them
Regretting the past they have lived

They walk together
Near the Forest of Lost Hope
Sickened by the ground they have tread
Desiring

Searching for the River Valley
A place to rest

Elizabethan II

260

*I*met a woman on the train
A woman of beauty and power

The woman glided to where I sat
Hiding in demurity
She engaged my feeble innocence
Disguised in eyes of purity

She whispered beauty to my mind
Caging me to her desire
My hope faded as she led me away
To my body's final hour

Adorned in lovely flowered attire
She took my hand of naivite
Leading me from my destination
To a place of sensuality

A creature of gentility
Imprisoning my soul
She led me to her rooming bed
To my final place of rest

Jonathan Lovejoy

Though I braved her storm of beauty
She flowed through my resistance
Haunting it with her insistence
Bringing it to naught

She removed my garment delicately
Pinning me to her sinning bed
In our Love she changed into a monster…
Clawing me to bloody death

I met a woman on the train
A woman of beauty and power
Hope faded when she led me away
To my body's final hour

261

Inside the house of poverty
Beside the road to nowhere
I heard the sound of a passenger train
Speeding towards eternity

I opened the curtain to my poverty room
To look into the dark of night
I saw the silver passenger train
Speeding down the road

Not a single track was laid
Upon this road to nowhere
But the train rolled on under cloak of night
Heading to infinity

A train arose from the dark of night
Speeding to eternity

262

In the halls of learning

Arises the need for fervent prayer

As terror moves from room to room

In a killing mood

51st Assembly

263

Demons call from the high wire

Snakes crawl from the mouth of the clown

Hide your children and lock the door

When this circus comes to town

264

A dual precipice
Threatens both sides of living
Pulling…
Seeking to pull a soul to its death

Along comes the addled
The otherworldly
Knowing nothing of where to go
Or what to do

Jonathan Lovejoy

265

DON'T mess around with Cathador

Burning in the Ring of Fire

Seething with hot lashes

From a life and time of suffering

Whereas out turns into whereas in

Where insane strivings begin

Inane drivings for perfection

Unable to achieve

266

Wallbacks skim the surface of contempt

Whispering trees of devastation

Whispering leaves of consecration

Whispering lies

Turning towards insanity's plea

A cry for mercy

From the bowels of suffering

From the depths

Jonathan Lovejoy

267

HELP laughter win

In the days of Noah

But tears and sorrow will rule

In the fire deluge

In their cataclysm of flame

No repentance can be given, no reprieve

Eat, drink, and be merry!

Until the time has come

268

*B*TW... 69505

Numbers given in the apocalypse
Numbers to confound
To track movement

Hosts speed through the city
Through the burning city limits
Knowing nothing of the night time
The time of life

Bound, driven by the need to achieve
The burning lust for power
The desire for success and riches
The ire

Jonathan Lovejoy

52nd Assembly

269

Caught in the whirlwind of melancholy

Pulled around and around

Being thrown from one building to the other

By their drive for the climbing life

The high rise work and living

The high life

270

An enemy to the dispossessed

With no compassion for sympathy

Like the angel in white

Men help every perversion come to life

Giving them a name

A soul to inhabit

A heart to corrupt

271

All of it is better than saying

Only music is what we know

Milk it in the light year

Cut it 'til the tears fall away

Do not save it for a rainy day

It breathes

It lives

It dies

272

Why are you looking for Him

You will never find Him in the weeds

In the garden of sin

Historical, hysterical winking with a nod

Thank them

For putting you out of your misery

Your suffering

Your dying

Jonathan Lovejoy

Elizabethan II

53rd Assembly

273

CRYSTALS sing

Screaming a new phrase…a new melody

Dominos made of glass
Packed together as one
One domino touches the other
Making it fall

A chirping sound emanates
The crystals all fall together
Raising a sound too loud to bear
Whistling to pierce the mind

Beware the Whistling Dominos
The slippery slope, causing one to fall
So that all will fall alongside
Into chaos

274

The sign of his coming
Lays horizontal across the sky
The Cross born in perpetual sin
In the glow of the evening day

Twilight looms upon the hill
Imprints of this Divinity
Frozen in racing form
Streaking across the sky

Sunset bathes the world in violet
A hue born from a mountain flow
Rising over a lost soul
In mourning

275

Children playing

Squealing, running around

Lost in the fog of their youth

Growing

Maturing

Leaving the playground of hope and dreams

To travel the road to adulthood

The road to misery

276

Guardian angels

They live among us

Walking, talking

Appearing in our dreams

Hoping to warn of danger

To protect us from evil

Having no power to do more

Than what they have been told

Jonathan Lovejoy

54th Assembly

277

Voices arise from below

Striking fear directly through me

Terrifying my mind

My sanity

278

The name rides on winds of ineffectiveness

Losing the destination path

Rising high into the sky

Caught in the treetop branches

279

Tilling soil in the Poverty Field
A failure and his beloved wife
Having no expectation for a harvest yield
Accursed in this unrequited life

Broken stiletto heels
Useless in the Poverty Field
A man and his wife till the soil
Beneath a metal clothing wire

THEIR SON drifts from Nowhere's Land
Saying "you two will be alright"
Having no desire for his parent's life
In the Poverty Field

55th Assembly

280

Twins drift evil through the house

Seeking to confound

To deceive

To destroy those who live there

Identical evil

Duplicity

Hiding their intentions

Until the woman of the house is killed

281

Phantoms from the past appear

In a spirit of goodwill

Saying "continue what it is you do"

Until the tiding

282

BEWARE the dead man
He sits in seat no. 37
Bumride the doilies
Twisted by them

Hatfields harbor misery
McCoys harbor pain
Raining fiery bullets from Hell
On a rainy day

Crystal bubbles threaten to float
Carrying bourbon above the city
Exploding the Light Brigade
Carem chocolate rings

Fire forms in cotton cloudiness
Blue streaks along the way
Haggish mirth in Dropdom
Maggish birthday kingdom

Elizabethan II

Why do dead men rule
On street no. 37?
Why do dead men fly
In seat no. 37?

Jonathan Lovejoy

56th Assembly

283

HE SAID "Raindrops keep falling on my head"
That means my life is red
Burning in a wicked flame
Blue and black fire

The wicked way has been chosen
Consult the dead for advice
Let them lead the way
To the Gates of HELL

Demons know what to say
Whispering androgynies
Angels say it better
Whispering moralities

Kate Leegan is here—
You better hope she can't afford not to!

284

$\mathcal{B}$E A KNIFE threat in prison
To the other delinquent girls
From wayward street
Their happy heart and home

Seek till the nillyistic kills
Billyish uptillian rexillian skills
Pillian jillian maximillian still
Magnaminostical dip dilliosity

I believe in piano research myself
It can lead to good things
Like punctuality
Duality

Legality and rope burned banality
Caught and raised in briar stone
Homecookin' is homely lookin'
When the chef is on the phone...

Jonathan Lovejoy

Speaking lies
Repeating lies
Pies and Fries cry
Look a' there!

The Sheriff calls
Hug a bear!
Screaming from a mirror
A dark place

285

UNFORGETTABLE times—

Are buried in a grave

Shouting from beneath the soil:

"The girl with the cat eyes is dead!"

Pierced with hot bullets

Buried in the forest

A place of dread

286

ꞪØW is the Hootnanny doing this?

Where is the strength

It comes from high above

In the clouds of snow pain

Give me a lady, Hassah!

Candy kisses sweet—

In Lei's blue lace

Waiting for the dream to end

The nightmare

Harple spirits coming

Hearken to their needs

Spinning tops across the grass

The great lawn

What's that noise?

Great Scott!

How can you ask that?

You're the center of it!

Elizabethan II

The other doilies have no drive either
So what am I supposed to do about it?
Cumquat in the mellon patch!

These are funny when they happen
The ice pitages
The stage of niceness never lasts
When evil blasts its ugly through

Juggly, wuggly, puggly, muggly
Figgly, wiggly, jiggly pig

He brought him back to life
It was the way he did it that made it so good
Kitty is on the nervous side
About this thing blowing over

This ding
This ding-a-ling
This ring-a-ding ding-a-ling
Tingly

Rosalind caught it in the shoulder
Pee-awng!

57th Assembly

287

GOD will blind us

To the fullness of himself

Until that day

That hour

When the sky will split

And angels will pour in

Like a light

Falling to our last day

Our burning

Our choking death!

288

*D*on't go in the root cellar

You won't come out alive

Hobgoblins and the tragedy of existence

Hippo-cradle—

The door is shut on opportunity—

Everyone will suffer!

Jonathan Lovejoy

289

*I*NSIDE the ineffectual car

Stalled beside the road to nowhere

I sit humming a tune with the dead

Near the Land of Poverty

290

THE WORLD FAMOUS idiotic
Luminaric has tendencies
Hot-bagged on the Bootland Trail!
Left to die

Screams of ecstasy!
Screams of agony!
Sins passed through the Mother Line
Through the blood

A warning to the Daughters…
Do better!
A warning to the Sisters…
Don't let her!

Flee it when it comes
Disguised in Beauty and Perfume
Masculinity…
Femininity…

Death

Jonathan Lovejoy

58th Assembly

291

THE WIFE came to my poverty room

With news of a man she had seen before

She spoke to me in words of doom:

Saying "Your dead father is knocking at the door!"

292

CHOIRS sing feeble verses

On the Shores of the Apocalyptic Notion

Angels motion towards the dispossessed

Mocking them

Leaving them to wallow in scorn

In hopelessness

Grinding despair into their souls

Unmercifully

293

TWO among the privileged

The happy and well to do

Took turns mocking the young one's pain

His inexperience

Seeing his dreadful inadequacy

Saying *"The word is out on this young man!"*

He has no ability

No future

294

HØPE is a nice place to visit
But I wouldn't want to live there
The Grieving Land is my home
The place where I belong

Turning back at *aujourd' hui!*
Where the signpost appears up ahead
Corruption and filth are my companions
Despair is where I make my bed

Awakened by the bluebird song
Screeching through an open window
Calling forth my Days of Hell…
My devastation

Jonathan Lovejoy

295

Spirits speak in lying riddles

Seeking to confound

Conjured from the fires of Hell

To give false hope

59th Assembly

296

The Clown Allegretto

Exposition!

Pling…pling…pling…

Boo boo bool
Buh plinka-ta-pip, plinka-ta-pip
Plinka-ta-pip

Boo boo bool
Buh plinka-ta-pip, plinka-ta-pip
Plinka-ta-pip

Bah bah ball
Buh plinka-ta-pip, plinka-ta-pip
Plinka-ta-pip

Boo buddah-bool
Badda blinka-tinka plip…

PLING!

Elizabethan II

Development!

Ploo ploo ploo ploo ploo
Ploo ploo ploo ploo
Blee bling bling blong blong blong
Blee bling bling blong blong bloon...

Ploo ploo ploo ploo ploo
Ploo ploo ploo ploo
Pling plick pling plang plang plang
Plee plee pla ploon

Plee plee... pla ploon...

Recapitulation!

Boo boo bool
Buh plinka-ta-pip, plinka-ta-pip
Plinka-ta-pip

Boo boo bool
Buh plinka-ta-pip, plinka-ta-pip
Plinka-ta-pip

Bobble bobble bobble omulobble
Bop bop bop Bop
Bom boo-bong, boo-bong, boo-bong

Jonathan Lovejoy

Coda!

Poppa poppa poppa poppa
Poppa pop

Boppa boppa boppa boppa
Boppu bop...

PLANG!

297

YOU bloody bastian
Wisdom doesn't grow on trees
Or does it?

Wee Willy Wilcom…
Will you come out to play?

Today is your last day on earth
Be punctillyicious!
Be punctillious about it!
Scrumptious times lay ahead

Why are you resisting it?
Don't insist to be taken out feet first!
Billy will come and get you
When the time is right

Lucipher will touch you
If the crime is done at night

298

Demons!

Knocking at my door

Seeking to get in

But they are at the wrong door

They have gone away

To kill someone else!

To serial another child in waiting

To take another life

Their innocence

Their laughter creeps in through the walls…

Raking in upon waves of milling

Billing from days of filling time

Crimes committed upon the killing fields

Jumptillyistic nillying skills

Joked, choked upon the Ashes Main

Pain beyond your feeble brain

Agony past what you can abstain

Or endure, I suppose

Elizabethan II

Don't fight it!
Try not to blight it!
With all your might
Stop trying to slight it

It's coming against your will
You can't deny or delight it!
Try it!
Yes, you will be a corpse

Stop running!
It's fun!
Death is the best part…
The beginning

299

VOICES inside my head

Noises decry they stead

Choices defy thy fed

Boise will fry under the red sun

Shrimp are delicious!

Scrimptillyicious those

Umptollywoggs

Bogged down by human desire

Fires of lustful hate

Burning, boiling

Roiling flesh and churning

Learning which leads to burning

Spurning...

Journeying thru

Mr. Durning will have his evil way again

Until every part of conscious is dead

300

*T*here's a trick to it

The mind sees things the body cannot

Secret things

Glimpses into the next plane

Where voices live without bodies

Where consequences are made

Choices given

Yes, life is horror!

Stop beating around it!

Pain is in the mulberry bush

Waiting to sting your face

To blister your skin until you fry…

In the afterlife

Jonathan Lovejoy

301

Ghosts sing low
Then high once again
Moving up from the soil
Through the grass

Singing up to the highest treetops
Bound by the earthly plane
Afraid to go into the sky
These ghosts are real

Living among the living
Flowing back down from the treetops
To the grassy plain
Flowing to the first house they see

Moving through the walls of contempt
Seeing all things

302

Is there a message in the birdsong?
It is this...
Die gladly!

Listen to the whispering Death in the cold wind
It is your Honor for the asking
Your Gift for being born

Don't cry when it comes to get you
Fly!
Don't cry over spilt milk and blood...

Die, Soldier!

ABOUT THE AUTHOR

Jonathan Lovejoy is a graduate of the University of North Carolina at Greensboro, with a B.A. in Religious Studies. He currently lives in Winston Salem, North Carolina.

For more info on the author's life and career, visit jonathanlovejoy.com

www.ingramcontent.com/pod-product-compliance
Lightning Source LLC
Chambersburg PA
CBHW060918040426

42445CB00011B/679